Free Trade

Nicolas Brasch

Australia • Brazil • Japan • Korea • Mexico • Singapore • Spain • United Kingdom • United States

Free Trade

Text: Nicolas Brasch
Editor: Vanessa Pellatt
Design: Karen Mayo
Series design: James Lowe
Photo researcher: Lisa Piemonte
Production controller: Adam Bextream
Reprint: Siew Han Ong

Acknowledgements
The author and publisher would like to acknowledge permission to reproduce material from the following sources:
AAP Image/Julian Smith: p. 23; Alamy/Bill Lyons: p. 12; Corbis/Andrew Kent: p. 11; Getty Images: pp. 3, 5, 10, 15, 16, 17, 22 (inset), back cover; iStockphoto: pp. 4–5; iStockphoto/Dan Barnes: cover, p. 1; iStockphoto/Rafael Ramirez Lee: p. 6; iStockphoto/Robert Churchill: p. 18; Jupiterimages Corporation: p. 22 (main); Newspix/AFP: p. 9; Newspix/Tony Lewis: p. 20; Photolibrary/Peter Schmid: p.21; Photolibrary/Volker Steger: p. 14; Richard Morden © Cengage Learning Australia: pp. 7, 8, 13, 19.

Every effort has been made to trace and acknowledge copyright. However, if any infringement has occurred, the publishers tender their apologies and invite the copyright holders to contact them.

Fast Forward Independent Texts Level 21

For product information and technology assistance,
in Australia call 1300 790 853;
in New Zealand call 0508 635 766

For permission to use material from this text or product,
please email **aust.permissions@cengage.com**

ISBN 978 0 17 017995 9
ISBN 978 0 17 017899 0 (set)

Cengage Learning Australia
Level 7, 80 Dorcas Street
South Melbourne, Victoria Australia 3205

Cengage Learning New Zealand
Unit 4B Rosedale Office Park
331 Rosedale Road, Albany, North Shore NZ 0632

For learning solutions, visit **cengage.com.au**

Printed in Australia by Ligare Pty Ltd
2 3 4 5 6 7 22 21 20 19

Free Trade

Nicolas Brasch

Contents

Why Countries Trade

Trade occurs when goods and services are bought or sold. Countries trade goods and services because no country can produce all the things that its citizens need.

Trade between Australia and Japan is a good example of this. Australia is a big country with **ample** land for farming and lots of **minerals** in the earth.
Japan is a small country with very little land that is good for farming and very few minerals.
So Australia **exports** agricultural products and minerals to Japan.

The Japanese have developed technology that helps them to make motor vehicles and electronic goods more cheaply than Australian companies can. So Australia **imports** motor vehicles and electronic goods from Japan.

This car is being built in Japan by robotic equipment.

CHAPTER 2

Free Trade or Protection?

Free trade occurs when governments do not **restrict** trade between countries.

The opposite of free trade is protection. Protection is when governments try to protect their country's goods and services from outside competition. They try to keep jobs and profits in their own country.

Governments use **regulations** to protect their country's industries from foreign competition. These regulations include banning or restricting the movement of goods and services. When a government sets a ban, it refuses to let particular goods or services in or out of its country. A government can also restrict the amount of particular goods or services that are either imported or exported.

Up until 2004, Thailand protected its dairy industry through regulations. Now Australia and Thailand have a Free Trade Agreement and Australia exports dairy products to Thailand.

Tariffs are another way governments protect their country's products.
Tariffs are taxes that are put on imported goods and services.
These taxes make the imported items more expensive than the locally made ones.

Australia's tariffs on imported clothing are higher than its tariffs on other imported items.

While some countries support free trade, other countries prefer protection. Some countries use both systems.

There is no simple answer to whether free trade is the best system. Free trade has both advantages and disadvantages.

In 2004, American Trade Representative Robert Zoellick (right) and Australian Trade Minister Mark Vaile (left) signed a Free Trade Agreement.

CHAPTER 3

Advantages of Free Trade

One advantage of free trade is that it makes countries focus on trading the kinds of goods and services that they can produce cheaply and efficiently.
They need to be able to do this to compete in the global market and protect their own industries.

Goods and services that cost too much to produce are too expensive for consumers to buy.
Consumers could buy the same goods for a lower price from countries that produce those goods more efficiently.

a clothing factory in Sri Lanka

Example

A company in the USA makes television sets, selling them for $1 000.
In South Korea, a company makes and exports television sets, selling them for $800.
In this example, free trade gives people a choice.
They can choose to buy the less expensive, imported television set or the more expensive, locally made television set.

plasma television sets being built in South Korea

Fruit is exported from Jordan to the USA under their Free Trade Agreement.

Another advantage of free trade is that it allows companies to sell their goods and services to consumers in other countries without restrictions.

If countries did not trade with each other, then companies would only be able to sell to consumers in their own country.

For example, if an Australian company can't export its product, then the company's market is limited to people living in Australia.

But if it can sell to people in other countries, its **potential** market is much bigger.

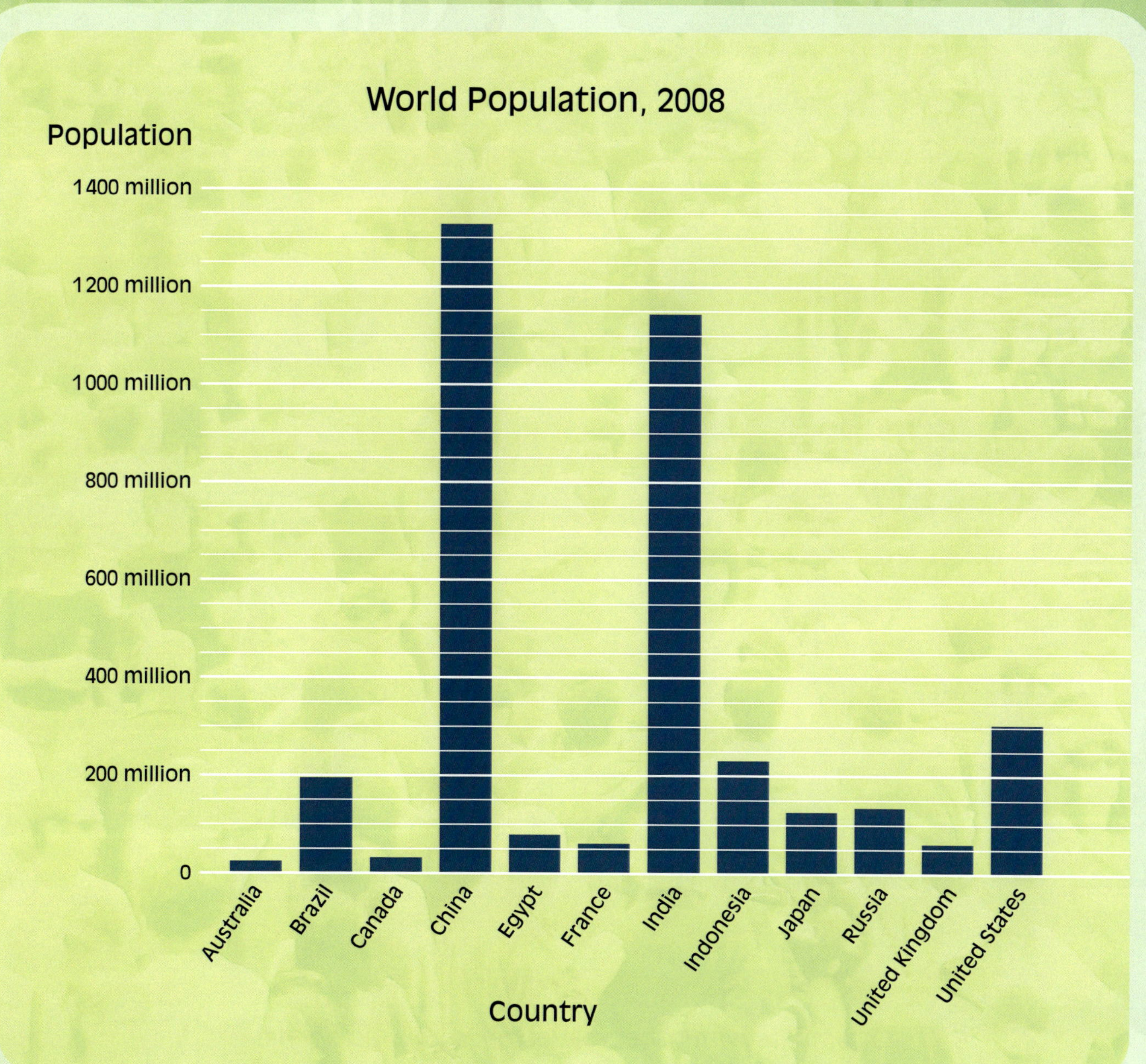

Free trade is good for consumers because companies must compete to produce goods and services more cheaply, making them cheaper to buy.

To compete with other toy factories, this factory has found ways to produce and export its toys very cheaply.

Free trade gives consumers more choice. They can buy goods and services that come from many different countries, not just products from their own country.

CHAPTER 4

Disadvantages of Free Trade

Free trade has some disadvantages, too.
One disadvantage is that some people lose their jobs because the company they work for closes down.
This happens when the goods that they make, or the services that they provide, are more expensive than imported goods and services.

More than 2000 workers lost their jobs when a car factory in England closed down.

For example, if Australia and Japan did not allow free trade, consumers in Australia would only be able to buy cars that were made in Australia.
This means that there would be lots of jobs in the Australian car industry.

But with free trade allowed, Australian consumers are able to buy cheaper cars that are made in Japan.
This means that the car industry in Australia does not produce as many cars and does not need as many workers.

a car assembly line in Japan

Another disadvantage is that **developing** countries find it very hard to compete when there is free trade. This is because they do not have the technology to produce goods and services as cheaply as the more developed countries can.

Without updated technology, it is difficult for this farmer to grow crops cheaply and efficiently.

When consumers in developing countries buy goods and services from countries with better technology, money flows out of the developing countries and into the richer countries.

Processed foods are often exported to developing countries.

Free trade means that some countries focus only on producing the small number of goods and services that they can make cheaply.

This can be bad if **demand** for these goods and services suddenly decreases.

Wool bales sit in a warehouse in Australia during a decrease in the demand for wool.

For example, the high cost of oil and the environmental damage caused by oil products mean that many countries are developing other energy sources.

If these countries choose to use different energy sources, they will not need to buy as much oil. Countries that mainly produce and sell oil will suddenly find that they have a product that is no longer in demand.

an oil field in Iraq

CHAPTER 5

Conclusion

Advantages of Free Trade

- Countries can compete globally by cheaply and efficiently producing goods and services.
- Companies can sell their goods and services to consumers in other countries without restrictions.
- Goods and services are cheaper.
- Consumers have more choice.

Disadvantages of Free Trade

- Some people lose their jobs.
- Money flows out of developing countries into richer countries.
- Countries that produce a small range of goods and services will have problems if demand decreases.

These workers lost their jobs when the factory they worked for was shut down.

Glossary

ample more than enough

demand the desire or need to purchase goods and services

developing in the early stages of becoming an industrial country

exports sends items to another country

imports brings items in from another country

minerals things such as coal or tin that are naturally formed in rocks and in the earth

potential capable of becoming something

regulations rules and controls

restrict put limits on something

Index